MICROSOFT
OUTLOOK
For Beginners

The Complete Guide To Learning All The Functions To Manage Emails,
Organize Your Inbox, Create Systems To Optimize Your Tasks, And
How To Stay Organized & Productive At Work (Computer/Tech)

OUTLOOK FOR BEGINNERS

The Complete Guide To Learning All The Functions To Manage Emails, Organize Your Inbox, Create Systems To Optimize Your Tasks, And How To Stay Organized & Productive At Work (Computer/Tech)

TABLE OF CONTENTS

INTRODUCTION

Microsoft Outlook is a widely used email client and personal information manager developed by Microsoft.

It is a part of Microsoft's Office suite and offers an extensive selection of tools for managing connections, emails, calendars, tasks, and other things. Microsoft Outlook has developed into a vital tool for both consumers and businesses due to its intuitive layout and powerful features.

The robust email management features of Microsoft Outlook are one of the main benefits of using it. It allows users to send, receive, and organize emails efficiently. It is simple to manage all of your messages in one location thanks to Outlook's support for multiple email accounts.

It offers advanced filtering options, search functionality, and the ability to create folders and rules to automatically sort incoming messages. Additionally, Outlook provides features like email signatures, automatic replies, and a robust spam filter to enhance productivity and communication. Apart from email, Microsoft Outlook serves as a comprehensive personal information manager.

It smoothly interacts with calendars, enabling users to manage their daily activities such as setting reminders and scheduling appointments. Outlook's calendar feature enables users to create and share calendars, send meeting invitations, and view multiple calendars simultaneously. It also has task management features that let users make lists of things to do, assign due dates, and monitor their progress.

Microsoft Outlook's user interface is made to be simple and easy to use. The main window consists of various components that help users navigate through different functionalities. The navigation pane on the left side provides quick access to mail, calendar, contacts, tasks, and other modules.

The main content area displays the selected module, such as the inbox or calendar view. The ribbon at the top contains commands and options for each module, making it easy to perform actions like composing emails, scheduling appointments, or creating contacts. Outlook also offers customizable views, themes, and layout options to personalize the interface according to individual preferences.

In conclusion, Microsoft Outlook is an effective email program and private data manager with a wealth of functions to boost performance and management. It's a good option for people and organizations trying to simplify communication and successfully manage their schedules because of its email management features, connectivity with tasks and calendars, and intuitive design. Whether you want to manage your to-do lists, keep track of your emails, or schedule appointments, Microsoft Outlook offers a comprehensive platform for all your interaction and administrative needs.

CHAPTER 1

SETTING UP MICROSOFT OUTLOOK

S etting up Microsoft Outlook can be a straightforward process that allows you to manage your email accounts efficiently.

The instructions below will walk you through the installation of the application, setting up email accounts, creating signatures, and creating automatic replies.

The first step is installing Microsoft Outlook on your computer. Purchasing a standalone edition or setting it up as an element of the Office software bundle are your two alternatives for doing this. Following the instructions that are given on the screen will allow you to go to setup once the installation is complete. Setting up your email profiles in Microsoft Outlook is the next step. Select the" File" tab after opening the program.

Select "Add Account" to initiate the setup wizard. Enter your email address and password, and Outlook will automatically try to configure the settings for popular email providers. In the event that the automatic setup is unsuccessful, you have the option of choosing the manual installation option, in which case your email provider's server settings must be entered.

Once your email accounts are configured, you can set up signatures to personalize your outgoing emails. Open Outlook and choose the "File" tab, then choose "Options," then click "Mail" in the left. Select "Signatures" from the list of options under "Compose messages."

From there, you may make new signatures, edit existing ones, and apply them to various email accounts. Your name, address, and any additional information you wish to submit are acceptable parts of your name. Additionally, you can set up automatic replies to inform others when you're unable to respond promptly.

In the "File" tab, select "Automatic Replies" to open the options menu. Here, you can create separate automatic replies for internal and external recipients, set a start and end time for the automatic replies, and customize the message content. Automatic answers are particularly useful when you're away from work, on vacation, or at a corporate function.

You can set up Microsoft Outlook using these guidelines to handle your email accounts more efficiently. Whether you're installing the application, configuring email accounts, or customizing signatures and automatic replies, Outlook provides a user-friendly interface that streamlines your email management experience. Enjoy the convenience and productivity that Microsoft Outlook offers for your communication needs.

CHAPTER 2

NAVIGATING THE

OUTLOOK INTERFACE

Microsoft Outlook is a powerful and widely used email and personal information management application.

Navigating its interface efficiently is essential for maximizing productivity. Mail, Calendar, Contacts, Tasks and Notes are the main components of the Outlook consumer program, and each one serves a specific purpose. Understanding these components is key to effectively managing your communication and scheduling.

The Mail component of Outlook is the primary feature used for sending, receiving, and organizing emails. It allows users to create, read, and reply to messages, as well as manage folders, filters, and rules to keep their inbox organized. With features like search and filters, users can quickly find specific emails or categorize messages based on various criteria.

The Calendar in Outlook provides a comprehensive tool for managing schedules, appointments, and events. Users can create new events, set reminders, invite others to meetings, and view their calendar in different layouts such as daily, weekly, or monthly. It also integrates with other Outlook components, allowing users to associate emails, tasks, and notes with specific calendar events.

Contacts in Outlook serve as a centralized address book, storing information about individuals or organizations. Users can create, edit, and categorize contacts, as well as link them to emails, appointments, or tasks. The contact list is a valuable resource for quickly accessing important information about colleagues, clients, or friends.

Tasks offer a way to manage and track to-do items and assignments. Outlook's Tasks component allows users to create tasks, set due dates, prioritize them, and track their progress. Tasks can be associated with specific projects, emails, or appointments, providing a comprehensive view of all pending work.

Outlook's Notes component enables users to create and store digital notes. Notes can be used to jot down ideas, reminders, or important information and can be categorized and organized for easy access. Notes can also be associated with other Outlook components, making them an integral part of managing information.

Customizing the layout and views of the Outlook interface allows users to tailor it to their specific preferences and needs. Outlook offers various customization options, including changing the theme, rearranging toolbars, and adjusting the reading pane. Users can also customize views within each component, such as sorting emails by date or sender, choosing different calendar layouts, or grouping tasks by priority.

In conclusion, mastering the Microsoft Outlook interface involves understanding its main components, including Mail, Calendar, Contacts, Tasks, and Notes. These components offer comprehensive tools for managing emails, schedules, contacts, tasks, and notes.

Customizing the layout and views further enhances the user experience, allowing individuals to personalize the interface to suit their preferences and optimize their productivity. With a solid grasp of these features and customization options, users can navigate Outlook with ease and efficiently manage their communication and information management needs.

CHAPTER 3
MANAGING EMAILS IN
MICROSOFT OUTLOOK

Managing emails in Microsoft Outlook involves various tasks such as reading and composing emails, organizing emails into folders, and using filters and search to find specific emails. These features help users efficiently handle their email correspondence and stay organized.

This chapter will explore five key aspects of managing emails in Microsoft Outlook.

The first step in managing emails in Outlook is reading and composing emails. Outlook provides a user-friendly interface that allows users to view and respond to emails effortlessly. The reading pane displays the contents of an email, allowing users to quickly review and take action on messages.

Composing emails is also simple, with intuitive formatting options and the ability to attach files or add signatures. Outlook ensures a smooth email experience, enabling users to stay on top of their inbox. Another crucial aspect of managing emails is organizing them into folders.

Outlook offers a robust folder system that allows users to categorize and store emails based on different criteria. Users can create folders for specific projects, clients, or categories and move emails into these folders with a simple drag-and-drop action. This organization method helps users find and retrieve important emails easily, reducing clutter in the inbox and enhancing productivity.

Filters and search functionalities are invaluable tools for managing emails efficiently. Outlook provides a range of filtering options that enable users to sort emails based on criteria such as sender, subject, or date. By setting up filters, users can automatically direct specific emails to designated folders, reducing the need for manual organization.

Additionally, Outlook's powerful search feature enables users to locate emails quickly by using keywords, sender names, or other search parameters. These tools save time and streamline the process of finding relevant emails. In addition to folders and filters, Outlook also offers features like rules and flags that further enhance email management.

Rules allow users to automate specific actions based on predefined criteria. For example, users can create a rule to automatically mark emails from a specific sender as important or move emails with specific keywords to a designated folder. Flags, on the other hand, allow users to mark emails for follow-up or set reminders, ensuring important messages receive timely attention.

These additional features contribute to a more streamlined and organized email workflow. Lastly, Outlook provides integration with other Microsoft products and services, which expands its functionality and enhances email management. Users can sync their Outlook calendar with their email, allowing them to schedule appointments and meetings directly from their inbox.

Integration with OneDrive enables users to share large files or collaborate on documents seamlessly. Outlook is also accessible from a variety of devices, allowing users to handle their emails even on the road. As a result, Outlook is a flexible and practical solution for email management.

In conclusion, managing emails in Microsoft Outlook involves various features and functionalities that enable users to read, compose, organize, and search for emails effectively. With intuitive interfaces for reading and composing emails, a robust folder system for organization, and powerful filtering and search options, Outlook provides a comprehensive solution for email management. Additional features like rules, flags, and integration with other Microsoft products further enhance productivity and efficiency. By leveraging these tools, users can stay organized, save time, and streamline their email workflow with ease.

CHAPTER 4
ORGANIZING YOUR INBOX WITH FOLDERS AND CATEGORIES

Organizing your inbox with folders and categories in Microsoft Outlook can significantly improve your email management and productivity.

By creating and managing folders, applying categories to emails, and using rules to automatically organize incoming messages, you can keep your inbox neat and find important emails quickly.

Here are five paragraphs explaining these features in detail:

Creating and managing folders:

Microsoft Outlook allows you to create folders to categorize and store emails based on different criteria. Simply perform a right-click on the mailbox icon, choose "New Folder," and then provide a name.

You can create folders for specific projects, clients, or topics. Managing folders involves moving emails into appropriate folders manually or by using rules. By organizing your emails into folders, you can declutter your inbox and easily locate messages when needed.

Applying categories to emails:

Categories are color-coded labels that you can assign to emails to visually differentiate them based on their importance, type, or any other criteria you define. To apply a category, select the email, go to the "Categorize" button in the Ribbon, and choose the desired category or create a new one.

Categories can help you quickly identify and prioritize emails. For example, you can assign a "High Priority" category to urgent emails or use different categories for different projects or departments.

Using rules to automatically organize incoming messages:

Outlook's rules feature allows you to automate the process of organizing incoming emails. Various activities can be performed by rules depending on predetermined criteria.

For instance, you can create a rule that automatically moves emails from a particular sender to a specific folder, or apply a category to emails containing specific keywords. To create a rule, go to the "File" tab, select "Manage Rules & Alerts," and set up your desired conditions and actions. Rules save time by automatically sorting your incoming messages, keeping your inbox organized.

Using sub-folders and subclasses to streamline your workflow in addition to building major folders will help you better manage your emails. Subfolders allow you to create a hierarchical structure within your main folders.

For instance, you could make sub-folders for each customer's name inside of a "Clients" folder. Similarly, subcategories enable you to create a more detailed classification system within your categories. This additional level of organization can help you navigate through your emails more efficiently and maintain a clear overview of your inbox.

Managing and archiving emails:

Regularly managing and archiving your emails is essential to prevent your inbox from becoming cluttered. Microsoft Outlook provides the option to manually or automatically archive emails based on specified criteria, such as date or folder.

Archiving moves older emails to separate folders, allowing you to access them when needed while keeping your active inbox clean. By archiving messages, you can free up storage space and maintain a streamlined email management system.

In conclusion, utilizing folders, categories, and rules in Microsoft Outlook is an effective way to organize your inbox and improve productivity. By creating folders, applying categories, and using rules, you can streamline your email workflow, find messages quickly, and maintain a clutter-free inbox. Taking the time to set up these organizational features can significantly enhance your email management experience in Outlook.

CHAPTER 5

MANAGING CONTACTS IN
MICROSOFT OUTLOOK

Managing contacts in Microsoft Outlook provides a convenient way to stay organized and efficiently communicate with individuals and groups.

Users may easily add, modify, and manage their contacts using a variety of features and capabilities in Outlook. Users can provide necessary information such name, email address, phone number, and any remarks while adding contacts, which is an easy process. The option to edit contacts ensures that information can be easily updated and modified as needed, providing an up-to-date record of important connections.

Organizing contacts into groups is a powerful feature of Microsoft Outlook, enabling users to categorize and manage their contacts efficiently. By creating contact groups, users can easily send emails, schedule meetings, or share information with specific subsets of contacts. This functionality proves particularly useful when dealing with large contact lists or when working on projects that involve multiple individuals.

With just a few clicks, users can select the desired group and communicate with all its members simultaneously. Another valuable aspect of managing contacts in Outlook is the ability to use contact lists for easy email distribution. Contact lists, also known as distribution lists or mailing lists, allow users to create a predefined group of contacts for streamlined communication.

Users can create a list containing the email addresses of clients, team members, or any other group of individuals they frequently correspond with. When sending an email, instead of manually adding each recipient's email address, users can simply select the contact list, saving time and reducing the chance of errors. In addition to email distribution, contact lists can be used for other purposes within Outlook.

For instance, users can use contact lists to invite a group of people to a meeting or to share a calendar with multiple individuals simultaneously. This versatility ensures that contact lists become a valuable tool for managing various types of interactions within the Outlook environment. Overall, Microsoft Outlook provides a comprehensive set of features for managing contacts effectively.

The ability to add and edit contacts ensures accurate and up-to-date information, while organizing contacts into groups simplifies communication with specific subsets of individuals. Additionally, the use of contact lists streamlines email distribution and facilitates efficient coordination within projects or teams. By leveraging these features, Outlook users can maintain a well-organized and streamlined approach to managing their contacts and improving their productivity.

CHAPTER 6

MANAGING APPOINTMENTS

IN OUTLOOK CALENDAR

Microsoft Outlook Calendar is a versatile tool that provides a seamless experience for scheduling and managing appointments.

Users may effectively arrange their daily tasks with its user-friendly layout and comprehensive features. One of the key functionalities is the ability to create and edit appointments effortlessly. Users can input essential details such as the event title, location, start and end times, and any additional notes.

Due to their ability to customize their meetings to meet their own needs, people are more able to honor their promises. Setting reminders and recurring events is another valuable feature offered by Outlook Calendar. By setting reminders, users can receive timely notifications to ensure they don't miss any important appointments or tasks.

Whether it's a pop-up alert or an email reminder, Outlook Calendar helps users stay organized and punctual. Recurring events are particularly useful for activities that repeat on a regular basis, such as weekly team meetings or monthly project reviews. With just a few clicks, users can set up these events to occur automatically, saving time and effort in manually creating them each time.

Outlook Calendar also facilitates seamless collaboration and coordination by enabling users to share their calendar with others. This feature is especially beneficial for teams, as it allows everyone to stay informed about each other's schedules. By granting specific permissions, such as viewing or editing rights, users can control the level of access others have to their calendar.

This enables efficient scheduling of meetings, ensuring that all attendees are available and aware of the event details. Sharing calendars fosters better communication and coordination, leading to increased productivity and streamlined workflows. Furthermore, Microsoft Outlook Calendar offers a range of customization options to enhance the scheduling experience.

Users can apply various colors and labels to appointments, making it easier to distinguish between different types of events. Additionally, Outlook Calendar allows users to set their availability status, such as "busy" or "out of office," which helps others understand their availability at a glance. These personalization features contribute to a more visually appealing and intuitive calendar interface, improving overall usability and organization.

In conclusion, Microsoft Outlook Calendar provides a comprehensive suite of features for scheduling and managing appointments. From creating and editing appointments to setting reminders and recurring events, the tool offers flexibility and convenience.

The ability to share calendars with others promotes collaboration and coordination, while customization options enhance the user experience. Whether used for personal or professional purposes, Outlook Calendar is a reliable and efficient solution for organizing one's schedule and ensuring that important appointments and tasks are not overlooked.

CHAPTER 7
COLLABORATION WITH
OUTLOOK CALANDAR

Collaboration with Microsoft Outlook Calendar offers a seamless and efficient way to manage schedules and coordinate with colleagues.

Scheduling meetings and inviting attendees has never been easier. Users may easily create new events, specify the day and time, and choose the required attendees from their contact database with only a few clicks.

Outlook Calendar then automatically sends out invitations to all attendees, making it effortless to coordinate everyone's availability. The system also allows users to include additional details, such as the meeting agenda or location, ensuring all participants are well-informed beforehand. Responding to meeting requests becomes a breeze with Outlook Calendar's intuitive interface.

When users receive an invitation, they can quickly accept, decline, or propose a new time if the suggested meeting slot conflicts with their schedule. This two-way communication streamlines the coordination process, eliminating back-and-forth emails and helping everyone stay on the same page. Additionally, Outlook Calendar automatically updates the status of the meeting on the attendees' calendars as responses come in, ensuring that everyone is aware of the confirmed attendees.

One of the standout features of Microsoft Outlook Calendar is its ability to view multiple calendars simultaneously. This function is particularly useful for individuals who have several work-related or personal commitments to manage. Users can overlay multiple calendars, such as their personal schedule, team members' schedules, or project-specific calendars, enabling them to gain a comprehensive overview of their day or week at a glance.

This feature promotes better time management and facilitates informed decision-making when scheduling new events or appointments. Collaboration through Outlook Calendar goes beyond the traditional email invitations. It integrates seamlessly with other Microsoft Office applications, such as Teams and SharePoint, allowing for a more interconnected and collaborative experience.

Users can access shared documents, chat with team members, and even conduct virtual meetings directly from the calendar interface.

This tight integration enhances teamwork and boosts productivity by providing a centralized platform for all collaboration needs. Moreover, Outlook Calendar's synchronization capabilities ensure that users stay updated across all devices.

Whether accessing the calendar from a desktop, laptop, smartphone, or tablet, changes made on one device reflect instantaneously on others. This mobility and real-time synchronization enable users to stay on top of their schedules, even when on the go. Overall, Microsoft Outlook Calendar's robust and user-friendly features make it an indispensable tool for efficient collaboration and time management in any professional setting.

CHAPTER 8

CREATING AND MANAGING

TASKS IN OUTLOOK

Microsoft Outlook is a potent application that enables you to easily create and manage projects in addition to helping you handle all of your messages and appointments.

Setting up tasks and to-do lists in Outlook is a straightforward process. By selecting the "Tasks" icon or by pressing the Ctrl + Shift + K keyboard shortcut, you may easily create a task.

Outlook provides various options to customize your tasks, such as setting due dates, adding reminders, and categorizing them for easy organization. By creating to-do lists within Outlook, you can prioritize and stay on top of your work effectively. In addition to managing your own tasks, Outlook enables you to assign tasks to others.

This feature is particularly useful for team collaborations and delegating responsibilities. Right-clicking the assignment, choosing "Assign Task," and providing the recipient's email address will allow you to assign it to a colleague. Outlook will automatically send an email notification to the assigned person, including all the relevant details.

By assigning tasks, you can ensure that everyone is aware of their responsibilities and keep track of progress collectively. Tracking task progress is essential for staying organized and meeting deadlines. Outlook provides a comprehensive view of all your tasks, allowing you to monitor their status easily.

If you access the task after it has been allocated to an individual, you may check the "Status" field to see how far along it is. Outlook offers different status options like "Not Started," "In Progress," and "Completed." By regularly updating task statuses, you can have a clear overview of ongoing work and identify any potential delays or bottlenecks.

To enhance task management in Outlook, you can take advantage of additional features like adding attachments, setting task priorities, and creating subtasks. Attaching relevant files to tasks allows you to keep all the necessary information in one place, ensuring easy access when needed.

Setting task priorities helps you focus on critical tasks and manage your workload effectively. You can simplify difficult activities into smaller, more manageable pieces by creating subtasks, which makes it simpler to monitor progress and accomplish objectives. Overall, Microsoft Outlook provides a robust platform for creating, assigning, and tracking tasks.

With its user-friendly interface and extensive features, Outlook streamlines task management and enhances productivity. By utilizing Outlook's capabilities, you can stay organized, collaborate effectively with colleagues, and ensure that tasks are completed on time. Whether you are working individually or as part of a team, Outlook's task management features are indispensable for efficient work management.

CHAPTER 9

TAKING NOTES WITH OUTLOOK NOTES

Microsoft Outlook Notes is a powerful and versatile tool that allows users to efficiently take notes, organize their thoughts, and stay productive across devices.

Creating and organizing notes in Outlook is a seamless process that can be easily integrated into your daily workflow. Simply open Outlook's Notes area, select "New Note," and begin typing to make a new note.

You can organize your notes using different categories or color-coding them, making it easy to find and access specific information when needed. The ability to add dates and reminders to notes also helps users stay on top of their tasks and deadlines. One of the standout features of Microsoft Outlook Notes is its capability to add attachments to notes.

This allows users to include relevant files, images, or documents alongside their written content, making the notes more comprehensive and useful. Whether you need to reference a presentation, link a related article, or attach an image for reference,

Outlook Notes supports various file types, streamlining your note-taking process and consolidating all relevant information in one place.

Syncing notes across devices is another invaluable aspect of using Microsoft Outlook Notes. With seamless synchronization across your desktop, smartphone, and tablet, you can access your notes anytime, anywhere. Your notes will always be accessible and up-to-date, whether you're on the move or WFH, letting you keep your concentration and productivity even while switching between devices.

The ability to share notes with colleagues or collaborators adds a collaborative dimension to Outlook Notes. You can easily send a note as an email or share it through a link, promoting efficient communication and cooperation in team settings. This feature fosters better information sharing, brainstorming, and task delegation, making Outlook Notes a valuable tool for both individual users and teams.

Lastly, the integration with Microsoft's broader ecosystem, such as OneDrive, further enhances the capabilities of Outlook Notes. By storing your notes in OneDrive, you can ensure data security, automatic backups, and seamless access from other Microsoft apps and services. This integration makes it easier to incorporate your notes into various tasks, ensuring that your valuable information is always at your fingertips.

In conclusion, Microsoft Outlook Notes is a comprehensive and efficient note-taking tool that offers a plethora of features to enhance productivity. From creating and organizing notes to adding attachments and seamless synchronization across devices, Outlook Notes ensures that you can easily capture and access essential information whenever and wherever you need it. Its collaboration features and integration with other Microsoft services further solidify its position as a top choice for individuals and teams looking to optimize their note-taking and organization processes.

CHAPTER 10
USING OUTLOOK'S SEARCH
AND FILTER FEATURES

Microsoft Outlook offers a wide range of search and filter features that greatly enhance productivity and help users efficiently manage their emails, contacts, and other items.

With the help of these tools, users can easily find particular emails, contacts, and other stuff. They may also do complex searches and filter emails according to predetermined criteria. One of the most valuable aspects of Outlook's search and filter features is the ability to find specific emails, contacts, and other items with ease.

With the help of Outlook's search functionality, you can easily find the needed data, whether you're looking for a certain message from an individual or a contact's mobile number. By simply entering relevant keywords or using specific search terms, you can narrow down your search and retrieve the necessary items promptly. In addition to basic search capabilities, Outlook provides advanced search options that further refine your search results.

These advanced search features enable users to specify various criteria, such as the sender, subject, date range, and even specific folders. By leveraging these options, you can perform targeted searches, saving time and effort. Whether you're looking for emails within a particular time frame or searching for attachments with specific file types, Outlook's advanced search options offer powerful tools to meet your needs.

Another valuable feature of Outlook is its ability to filter emails based on specific criteria. Users can instantly categorize and sort incoming emails with the aid of filters, which makes it simpler for them to manage and prioritize their inbox. Outlook allows you to create rules that filter emails based on sender, subject, keywords, or other conditions.

For example, you can set up a filter to automatically move emails from a specific sender to a designated folder or mark emails with specific keywords as important. These filters help streamline your email management process and keep your inbox organized. Moreover, Outlook's search and filter features extend beyond just emails.

Users can also search and filter contacts, calendar events, tasks, and other items within Outlook. This enables efficient management of various aspects of your professional and personal life. Whether you're trying to find a specific contact's information or searching for an important meeting in your calendar, Outlook's search and filter capabilities offer a comprehensive solution to easily locate and access the desired information.

Overall, Microsoft Outlook's search and filter features greatly enhance productivity and streamline email and item management. By leveraging these capabilities, users can find specific emails, contacts, and other items quickly, perform advanced searches with specific criteria, and filter emails based on various conditions. With Outlook's powerful search and filter functionality, users can effectively stay organized, save time, and focus on what matters most.

CHAPTER 11

MANAGING JUNK AND SPAM EMAILS

Managing junk and spam emails is an essential task when using Microsoft Outlook to ensure a clutter-free and organized mailbox. Outlook offers various features and settings that can help streamline this process.

This section will discuss three key aspects of managing junk and spam emails in Microsoft Outlook: configuring junk email settings, marking emails as junk or not junk, and blocking and unblocking senders.

Firstly, configuring junk email settings in Outlook is crucial to enhance the effectiveness of the built-in spam filter. By accessing the "Junk Email Options" menu, users can customize the level of protection and set filters based on their preferences.

They can choose to automatically move suspected junk emails to the Junk Email folder, block specific senders or domains, and even whitelist trusted contacts to ensure important emails are never marked as spam. Secondly, marking emails as junk or not junk is a simple yet effective way to train Outlook's spam filter and improve its accuracy.

Whenever a spam email manages to reach the inbox or a legitimate email is mistakenly flagged as junk, users can manually mark it as junk or not junk. Outlook will learn from these actions and apply the knowledge to future email filtering, gradually improving its ability to differentiate between wanted and unwanted emails.

In addition to marking individual emails, users can also block and unblock senders in Outlook. This feature comes in handy when dealing with persistent spammers or unwanted senders. By right-clicking on an email, selecting "Junk," and then choosing "Block Sender," users can prevent future emails from that sender from reaching their inbox.

Conversely, if a sender was mistakenly blocked or needs to be unblocked, users can access the "Blocked Senders" list in the Junk Email Options menu and make the necessary changes. Furthermore, Outlook's spam filter can be strengthened by regularly reviewing the contents of the Junk Email folder. While the filter is generally accurate, it is possible for legitimate emails to be caught in the spam net.

By periodically checking the Junk Email folder, users can identify any false positives and move them back to the inbox, ensuring no important communications are missed. Lastly, to further enhance spam management, users can take advantage of Outlook's integration with third-party email security solutions.

These solutions offer advanced spam detection and provide an additional layer of protection against sophisticated phishing attempts and malicious emails. By utilizing these tools in combination with Outlook's built-in features, users can achieve a robust defense against junk and spam emails, creating a safer and more efficient email experience.

In conclusion, managing junk and spam emails in Microsoft Outlook is crucial for maintaining an organized inbox. By configuring junk email settings, marking emails as junk or not junk, and blocking and unblocking senders, users can train Outlook's spam filter, keep unwanted emails at bay, and ensure important messages are not mistakenly flagged as spam.

Regularly reviewing the Junk Email folder and considering third-party email security solutions can further enhance spam management capabilities. With these practices in place, users can enjoy a clutter-free and secure email environment within Microsoft Outlook.

CHAPTER 12

CUSTOMIZING OUTLOOK'S APPEARANCE AND SETTINGS

C ustomizing Outlook's appearance and settings in Microsoft Outlook allows users to tailor the program to their preferences and enhance their productivity.

With a range of options available, users can make changes to the theme and layout, adjust email and calendar settings, and personalize their Outlook experience. These customization features provide a more personalized and efficient workflow.

One way to customize Outlook's appearance is by changing the theme and layout. Outlook offers various themes that can alter the color scheme and overall look of the interface. Users can choose a theme that suits their taste or aligns with their organization's branding.

Additionally, users can customize the layout by rearranging the different panes, such as the folder pane, reading pane, and navigation pane, to create a more intuitive and efficient workspace. Adjusting email and calendar settings is another essential aspect of customizing Outlook. Users can configure email settings to control how messages are displayed, organized, and sorted.

This includes setting up email signatures, creating rules for automatic message handling, and managing email storage and synchronization options. Similarly, users can customize calendar settings to define default meeting durations, working hours, and reminder notifications, enabling them to manage their schedules more effectively. Personalizing the Outlook experience goes beyond appearance and settings.

Outlook allows users to personalize their experience by adding shortcuts, customizing ribbons, and creating quick steps for repetitive tasks. Shortcuts provide quick access to frequently used folders, emails, or commands, while customizing ribbons allows users to organize the toolbar according to their preferences. Quick steps, on the other hand, automate repetitive actions by creating custom one-click commands, streamlining common tasks and saving time.

Furthermore, users can enhance their Outlook experience by integrating third-party add-ins and plugins. These additional tools offer extended functionality, such as email tracking, email templates, advanced email filtering, and project management integration. By selecting and installing the relevant add-ins, users can tailor Outlook to meet their specific needs and enhance their productivity.

In conclusion, customizing Outlook's appearance and settings empowers users to create a personalized and efficient email and calendar management system. Whether it's changing the theme and layout, adjusting email and calendar settings, or personalizing the overall Outlook experience, these customization options provide users with a tailored workflow that aligns with their preferences and boosts productivity. By leveraging the various customization features, users can optimize their Outlook experience and streamline their daily communication and scheduling tasks.

CHAPTER 13

USING OUTLOOK ON MOBILE DEVICES

U sing Outlook on mobile devices offers a convenient way to stay connected and organized while on the move. Setting up the Microsoft Outlook software on the device you're using is a simple procedure.

Users may set up their mailboxes quickly and begin viewing their emails from wherever after completing a few easy steps. The app supports various email providers, allowing users to easily integrate multiple accounts and streamline their communication. Syncing emails, contacts, and calendars is a crucial feature of Outlook on mobile devices.

Users can ensure that their email correspondence is synced across all of their devices once the application is configured. This means that emails read or deleted on a mobile device will reflect the same changes on other devices, such as a desktop or tablet. Additionally, contacts and calendars can also be synced, enabling users to access their important contacts and schedule on the go.

Managing Outlook on the go becomes effortless with the mobile app. Users can easily compose, reply to, and forward emails from their mobile devices. The intuitive interface of Outlook on mobile ensures a smooth and familiar experience, making it easy to navigate through different folders and search for specific messages.

Users can also organize their emails by creating folders, marking messages as important, or flagging them for follow-up, helping to prioritize and manage their inbox efficiently. The mobile version of Outlook offers several productivity-enhancing features. On their mobile devices, users may book and manage their appointments, create reminders, and get alerts for approaching events.

As a result of the app's flawless integration with the device's calendar and alert systems, users can remain on top of their plans and never forget a crucial appointment or deadline. Using the capabilities that the mobile app offers, people may maximize their time and become more productive. Utilizing Outlook on handheld gadgets also has the benefit of its interoperability with other Microsoft apps and services.

Users can access their OneDrive files, SharePoint documents, and Microsoft Teams conversations directly from the Outlook app. This integration provides a unified and seamless experience, allowing

44

users to access and manage all their Microsoft-related content from a single platform. It enables quick collaboration, document sharing, and efficient communication with colleagues, further enhancing productivity while on the go.

In conclusion, using Outlook on mobile devices offers numerous benefits, from easy configuration to seamless synchronization of emails, contacts, and calendars. With Outlook's mobile app, managing emails and staying organized becomes effortless, empowering users to be productive even when away from their desks.

The integration with other Microsoft services enhances the overall experience, providing a comprehensive platform for efficient communication and collaboration. Whether it's composing emails, scheduling appointments, or accessing important documents, Outlook on mobile devices is a powerful tool for professionals on the move.

CHAPTER 14
INTEGRATING OUTLOOK
WITH OTHER MICROSOFT APPS

Integrating Microsoft Outlook with other Microsoft apps offers a seamless experience for users, enhancing productivity and streamlining communication and collaboration.

Outlook and Microsoft Word, Excel, and PowerPoint, which provide a comprehensive set of tools for file creation, editing, sharing, are two of the most significant connections. Users can easily attach files from these applications directly to emails in Outlook, making it convenient to share important documents with colleagues or clients. When using Outlook with Microsoft Word, users can compose professional emails with ease.

They can draft emails in Word, taking advantage of its powerful editing features, such as spell-checking, grammar correction, and formatting options. By clicking the "Send to Mail Recipient" option in Word, users can automatically open a new email in Outlook with the Word document attached, simplifying the process of sharing and collaborating on documents. Similarly, Outlook integration with

Microsoft Excel allows users to send spreadsheets as attachments in emails.

This integration facilitates data sharing and analysis by enabling users to send financial reports, budget plans, or other Excel files directly from the application. By clicking the "Send to Mail Recipient" option in Excel, users can quickly attach the file to an Outlook email, ensuring seamless communication with colleagues or clients. Outlook's integration with Microsoft PowerPoint offers a convenient way to share presentations and gather feedback.

Users can attach PowerPoint files to emails and send them directly from Outlook, making it effortless to distribute slideshows to team members or stakeholders. This integration enables collaboration on presentations, as users can easily request input, suggestions, or edits by sharing PowerPoint files through Outlook. Collaborating on documents through Outlook is made efficient with the integration of Microsoft apps.

By attaching files from Word, Excel, or PowerPoint to emails in Outlook, users can collaborate with others in real-time. They can share documents for review or editing, and recipients can open and modify the files directly, all within the familiar Outlook interface. This integration promotes seamless teamwork, allowing multiple individuals to work on the same document simultaneously, fostering productivity and enabling efficient collaboration.

In conclusion, combining Outlook by Microsoft with other software from Microsoft like Word, Excel, and PowerPoint boosts productivity by giving users access to a wide range of tools for creating, modifying, and sharing documents. These integrations streamline communication by allowing users to attach files from these applications directly to emails in Outlook.

Additionally, collaborating on documents becomes effortless through Outlook, as team members can share files, gather feedback, and work together in real-time. The integration of Outlook with Microsoft apps contributes to a seamless and efficient workflow, enabling users to maximize their productivity and collaboration efforts.

CHAPTER 15

MANAGING EMAIL ATTACHMENTS

M anaging email attachments in Microsoft Outlook involves various tasks such as opening and saving attachments, sending attachments in emails, and managing attachment size limits.

These functionalities are essential for effective communication and file sharing. Outlook offers user-friendly features and options to streamline these processes, enhancing productivity and efficiency.

When it comes to opening and saving attachments in Outlook, the process is straightforward. Users can easily open an attachment in Outlook by clicking it when they receive an email with one. Users can also decide to" Save As" the attachment by right-clicking it and doing so.

This enables users to store attachments in a desired folder or location for future reference or use. Sending attachments in emails is another common task in Outlook. Users can easily attach files to their outgoing messages by clicking on the "Attach File" button within the email composition window.

This allows them to browse their computer's file system and select the desired attachment. Outlook also provides the option to attach files from cloud storage services such as OneDrive, making it convenient to share large files without overloading email servers. Managing attachment size limits is crucial to ensure efficient email delivery and avoid unnecessary delays.

Outlook has predefined attachment size limits that restrict the maximum size of attachments that can be sent or received. These limits are set by the email provider or system administrator. Outlook offers alternatives like compressing the file, sending it to a service that offers cloud storage, or breaking it up into numerous smaller pieces if the attachment is too large.

This helps users stay within the attachment size limits and ensures smooth email communication. In addition to managing attachment size limits, Outlook also offers features to help users track and organize attachments. The "Attachments" view in Outlook allows users to see all the attachments they have received or sent in a specific folder or conversation.

This view provides a quick overview of the files exchanged, making it easier to locate specific attachments or review the history of shared files. Users can also use search filters to find attachments based on file types, dates, or other criteria, further enhancing attachment management capabilities. To enhance security, Outlook incorporates various measures to protect against malicious attachments.

It automatically scans attachments for potential threats, such as viruses or malware, before opening or saving them. If a suspicious attachment is detected, Outlook may display a warning or prevent the file from being opened altogether. These security features ensure that users can safely manage email attachments without compromising their system's integrity or privacy.

In summary, managing email attachments in Microsoft Outlook involves opening and saving attachments, sending attachments in emails, and managing attachment size limits. Outlook provides user-friendly features for these tasks, allowing users to efficiently handle attachments, enhance productivity, and ensure secure file sharing. With its intuitive interface and robust attachment management capabilities, Outlook remains a popular choice for managing email communications in various personal and professional settings.

CHAPTER 16

USING OUTLOOK'S ADVANCED EMAIL FEATURES

M icrosoft Outlook offers a range of advanced email features that can enhance productivity and organization. One such feature is the ability to flag and categorize emails.

With flagging, users can mark important messages or tasks for follow-up, ensuring that they don't get overlooked. This feature is particularly useful for prioritizing emails and staying on top of important deadlines. Categorizing emails allows users to assign specific labels or tags to messages, enabling easy sorting and filtering.

By utilizing these features, Outlook users can maintain an efficient and well-organized inbox. Another valuable feature in Microsoft Outlook is the ability to set up email templates. Templates are pre-designed email formats that can be saved and reused for repetitive or commonly sent messages.

Whether it's a standard response, a meeting invitation, or a sales pitch, templates can save significant time and effort. Users can create and customize templates to suit their specific needs, streamlining communication and ensuring consistency across emails. This feature is especially beneficial for individuals who frequently send similar types of messages.

Creating and managing email signatures is another advanced feature offered by Microsoft Outlook. An email signature is a personalized block of text that is automatically added at the end of outgoing emails. It typically includes the sender's name, contact information, and additional details like job title or company logo.

Outlook allows users to create multiple signatures and choose different ones for various email accounts or message types. This feature helps in creating a professional and consistent email appearance while providing essential information to recipients. In addition to flagging, categorizing, email templates, and signatures, Outlook provides various other advanced features to enhance the email experience.

For example, users can utilize advanced search options to quickly find specific emails based on keywords, sender, date, or other criteria. The email rules feature enables automated actions like moving specific messages to designated folders, forwarding emails to other recipients, or marking them as read.

These features allow for efficient email management, saving time and reducing clutter in the inbox. Furthermore, Outlook's advanced features also extend to email organization and management. Users can create and customize folders to categorize and store emails based on projects, clients, or any other desired criteria.

With features like conversation view, users can group related messages together, making it easier to track and follow email threads. Outlook also offers robust spam and junk email filtering options to help reduce unwanted messages. By utilizing these features, Outlook users can maintain a streamlined and organized email workflow.

Overall, Microsoft Outlook's advanced email features, including flagging and categorizing emails, setting up email templates, creating and managing email signatures, advanced search options, email rules, and organization tools, empower users to streamline their email communication and stay organized. Users can gain productivity, save time, and manage their email correspondence more successfully by utilizing these capabilities.

CHAPTER 17
MANAGING MULTIPLE EMAIL
ACCOUNTS IN OUTLOOK

Managing multiple email accounts in Microsoft Outlook can be a convenient and efficient way to handle different aspects of your personal and professional life.

Outlook offers several features that facilitate the management of multiple accounts, including adding and switching between email accounts, setting up email forwarding and aliases, and managing account settings. Firstly, adding and switching between email accounts in Microsoft Outlook is straightforward.

You can easily link multiple email accounts, such as Gmail, Yahoo, or Exchange, to Outlook. By adding these accounts, you can access and manage all your emails from a single platform. Switching between accounts is as simple as clicking on the account name or profile picture, allowing you to effortlessly navigate between your different email addresses and consolidate your communications.

Secondly, Outlook enables users to set up email forwarding and aliases. Email forwarding allows you to automatically redirect emails received in one account to another account. This feature is particularly useful if you prefer to centralize your email management or want to consolidate notifications in a single inbox.

Additionally, aliases provide an effective way to manage multiple email addresses within a single account. You can create aliases for different purposes, such as personal, work, or online subscriptions, and manage them all from a unified interface. Furthermore, Microsoft Outlook offers extensive options for managing account settings.

You can customize various settings according to your preferences and organizational needs. For example, you can configure notifications to receive alerts only for specific accounts or folders. You can also set up automatic replies or out-of-office messages for individual accounts, ensuring that people contacting you receive timely and appropriate responses.

Furthermore, you can adjust synchronization settings to control how often Outlook checks for new emails or updates folders across your various accounts. Moreover, to these functions, Outlook offers an all-encompassing inbox view that compiles emails from multiple profiles into a single user interface.

As a result, you can rapidly scan and sort your communications without switching between accounts. Moreover, Outlook's robust search functionality enables you to efficiently locate specific emails or conversations across all your linked accounts, saving you time and effort in managing and retrieving important information.

In conclusion, Microsoft Outlook offers powerful tools for managing multiple email accounts. By adding and switching between accounts, setting up email forwarding and aliases, and customizing account settings, you can streamline your email management and enhance productivity.

Outlook's unified inbox and search capabilities further simplify the process, allowing you to efficiently handle communications across various email addresses from a single platform. Outlook gives users these tools so they can effectively manage both their personal and business email accounts, giving them a simplified and well-organized email experience.

CHAPTER 18
IMPROVING PRODUCTIVITY
WITH SHORTCUTS AND TIPS

I mproving productivity in Microsoft Outlook is essential for managing busy schedules and efficiently handling emails and tasks. Using keyboard shortcuts for frequent tasks is one of the best methods to increase productivity.

Instead of relying solely on the mouse, using keyboard shortcuts allows users to navigate through Outlook quickly. Simple shortcuts like Ctrl + N for creating a new email, Ctrl + Shift + I for marking an email as read, or Ctrl + Shift + B for opening the Address Book can save significant time throughout the workday.

Learning and incorporating these shortcuts into daily routines can streamline email management and enhance overall productivity. In addition to keyboard shortcuts, applying time-saving tips and tricks can make a substantial difference in Outlook's efficiency. For instance, utilizing the "Quick Steps" feature allows users to automate repetitive actions.

Users can set up custom Quick Steps for tasks like moving emails to specific folders, forwarding messages to colleagues, or categorizing emails for easier organization. By automating these processes, people may concentrate on more crucial aspects of their work and free up more time for simpler tasks. Customizing Outlook for maximum efficiency is another key strategy to enhance productivity.

Users can tailor the Outlook layout to suit their workflow preferences, such as arranging the layout to prioritize specific folders, calendars, or task lists. Furthermore, leveraging the power of Outlook's rules and filters can automatically sort incoming emails into relevant folders, reducing clutter in the main inbox and facilitating better email management. Integrating Outlook with other productivity tools can also contribute to improved efficiency.

Users can synchronize their Outlook calendar with other applications like Microsoft Teams or Google Calendar, ensuring they have a centralized view of their schedule and avoid double-booking or missing important appointments. Similarly, integrating task management tools like Microsoft To-Do or Trello can help organize and prioritize tasks within Outlook, ensuring no crucial task falls through the cracks.

Last but not least, keeping up with Outlook's most recent features and upgrades can increase productivity. Microsoft frequently adds new features and functionalities to the program with the goal of enhancing user experience and accelerating workflows. Regularly exploring these updates and learning how to use them effectively can provide users with an edge in maximizing their productivity with Microsoft Outlook.

In conclusion, using keyboard shortcuts for common tasks, applying time-saving tips and tricks, customizing the Outlook layout, integrating it with other productivity tools, and staying informed about updates are all valuable strategies for improving productivity with Microsoft Outlook. By implementing these techniques, users can manage their emails and tasks more efficiently, saving time and energy that can be redirected to more critical aspects of their work or personal life.

CHAPTER 19

STAYING ORGANIZED WITH OUTLOOK

S taying organized and productive at work is crucial for professionals to manage their tasks efficiently and achieve their goals.

Microsoft Outlook, a popular email and calendar application, offers a comprehensive set of tools and features that can significantly boost productivity. By utilizing Outlook as a task manager, individuals can streamline their workflow and ensure that important assignments are completed on time. Outlook's task management system allows users to create, prioritize, and categorize tasks, set due dates, and even delegate tasks to others.

This enables users to have a clear overview of their responsibilities, helping them stay focused and on track. Implementing the "inbox zero" technique is another effective way to stay organized using Microsoft Outlook. The inbox zero approach encourages users to keep their email inboxes empty or near-empty by consistently processing incoming messages.

By sorting emails into appropriate folders, archiving or deleting irrelevant messages, and promptly responding to critical emails, professionals can avoid clutter and reduce the chances of important information getting buried in a sea of unread messages. This approach can significantly reduce stress, save time, and enhance overall productivity. Leveraging Outlook's productivity features can also revolutionize work management.

The application provides powerful calendar tools that allow users to schedule and manage appointments, meetings, and deadlines effectively. By setting reminders and syncing Outlook with other devices, professionals can receive timely notifications, ensuring they never miss a crucial event or deadline. Moreover, the ability to share calendars with colleagues fosters collaboration and facilitates coordination within teams, leading to smoother project execution.

Furthermore, Outlook's integration with Microsoft's suite of productivity tools, such as Microsoft Teams and OneDrive, further enhances work management. With Teams, professionals can conduct virtual meetings, collaborate on documents in real-time, and exchange ideas seamlessly. OneDrive integration allows users to store, access, and share files securely from any device, promoting better organization and accessibility of essential documents.

In conclusion, Microsoft Outlook offers a robust platform for professionals to stay organized and productive at work. By utilizing it as a task manager, implementing inbox zero techniques, and leveraging its integration with other productivity features, individuals can optimize their work processes, efficiently manage their time, and ultimately achieve higher levels of productivity. Embracing these practices can lead to more focus, reduced stress, and a more successful and fulfilling professional life.

CONCLUSION

Microsoft Outlook is a popular email and personal information manager developed by Microsoft Corporation. Thousands of customers and companies depend on it because of its straightforward design and consistent performance.

One of Microsoft Outlook's many advantages is its compatibility with another Office programs from Microsoft like Word, Excel, and PowerPoint. This enables seamless management of emails, contacts, calendars, and tasks within a unified platform, streamlining workflow and enhancing productivity.

Pros of Microsoft Outlook include its robust email management capabilities, allowing users to organize their messages efficiently through folders, tags, and filters. The email threading feature helps keep conversations coherent and easy to follow. Furthermore, customers that want mobile access to their data will find it handy thanks to Outlook's interface with Exchange Server, which enables seamless synchronization of emails, calendars, and contacts across various devices.

However, like any software, Microsoft Outlook also has its cons. The UI could be too complex for some users, especially if they simply need the most basic email features. Additionally, Outlook can be resource-intensive, particularly when dealing with large email databases, leading to slower performance on older or less powerful machines.

Second, while it works beautifully with other Microsoft Office programs, utilizing it with non-Microsoft programs may not work as well, which may lead to compatibility concerns. To enhance workflow and productivity, Microsoft Outlook can be combined with various third-party applications. For instance, users can integrate it with task management tools like Microsoft To-Do or Trello to better organize their daily tasks and deadlines.

Additionally, project management software such as Asana or Monday.com can be linked with Outlook, allowing for smoother collaboration among team members. CRM systems like Salesforce or HubSpot can also be integrated, enabling businesses to maintain better customer relationships. The Microsoft Office package, which also comprises Word, Excel, and PowerPoint, contains Microsoft Outlook.

Microsoft offers a variety of pricing options, such as the one-time pay for one device and the subscription-based strategy known as Office 365, which gives customers access to the most recent versions of Microsoft Office programs across various devices and includes virtual backups and extra features.

Microsoft Outlook is anticipated to keep developing in the future to meet the shifting needs of users. Users may find it simpler to prioritize their communications as a result of advances in machine learning and artificial intelligence-based email filtering.

Additionally, enhanced integrations with emerging communication platforms and collaboration tools could further streamline workflow and foster better connectivity in the professional environment. Outlook will probably continue to be a major player in the field of email and private data administration space for generations to come thanks to Microsoft's dedication to ongoing development.

Printed by BoD™in Norderstedt, Germany

9 798223 619383